DIFFICULT RIDDLES FOR 10 Years Old Kids

300 RIDDLES AND BRAIN TEASERS THAT KIDS AND FAMILIES WILL LOVE!

OSCAR BALES

CONTENTS

DIFFICULT RIDDLES..5

DIFFICULT MATH RIDDLES...........................73

DIFFICULT VISUAL RIDDLES........................78

DIFFICULT RIDDLES ANSWERS.....................84

DIFFICULR MATH RIDDLES ANSWERS........111

DIFFICULT VISUAL RIDDLES ANSWERS......115

INTRODUCTION

" *Developing inner values is much like physical exercise. The more we train our abilities, the stronger they become. The difference is that, unlike the body, when it comes to training the mind, there is no limit to how far we can go.* "

Dalai Lama

This book is a collection of 300 brain teasing riddles and puzzles.Their purpose is to make children think and stretch the mind. They are designed to test logic, lateral thinking as well as memory and to engage the brain in seeing patterns and connections between different things and circumstances.

DIFFICULT RIDDLES

1. The shorter I am, the bigger I am. What am I?

2. What is bought by the yard by is worn by the foot?

3. With pointed fangs it sits in wait, with piercing force it doles out fate, over bloodless victims proclaiming its might, eternally joining in a single bite What is it?

4. What has a foot but no leg?

5. What stinks when living and smells good when dead?

6. What takes hours to pull off Is most satisfying when it's done and requires consent from the person, you're doing it to?

7. **What has a big mouth, yet never speaks?**

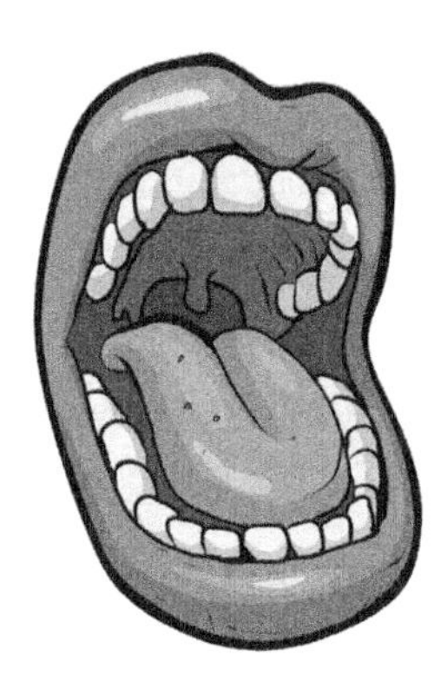

8. **The more you take the more you leave behind.**

9. **The virgin gave birth to a child and threw away the blanket.**

10. **There is a creature of God whose body is hard; it does not wish to eat unless you strike its head.**

11. **I have three hundred cattle, with a single nose cord.**

12. What do you have when you're sitting down that you don't have when you're standing up?

13. First you see me in the grass dressed in yellow gay; next I am in dainty white, then I fly away. What am I?

14. Born of sorrow, grows with age, you need a lot to be a sage. What is it?

15. Patch upon patch, without any stitches, if you tell me this riddle, I'll give you my breeches.

16. Some are quick to take it. Others must be coaxed. Those who choose to take it gain

and lose the most.

17. I go in dry and come out wet, the longer I'm in, the stronger I get. What am I?

18. No thicker than your finger when it folds. As thick as what it's holding when it holds.

19. I work hard most every day, not much time to dance and play, If I could reach what I desire, all like me would now retire. What am I?

20. Begotten, and born, and dying with noise, the terror of women, and pleasure of boys, Like the fiction of poets concerning the wind, I'm chiefly unruly, whenstrongestconfined.

21. They can be harbored, but few hold waters, you can nurse them, but only by holding

them against someone else, you can carry them, but not with yourarms,you can burythem, but not in the earth.

22. Full of dark, filled with everything Both

on my skin they color with my pack, I am always Afraid of the cat. What am I?

23. What goes up, but at the same time goes down? Up toward the sky, and down toward the ground. Its present tense and past tense too, come for a ride,justyouandme!

24. We travel much, yet prisoners are, and close confined to boot. Yet with any horse, we will keep the pace, and will always go on foot. What are they?

25. I bubble and laugh and spit water in your face. I am no lady, And I don't wear lace.

26. When the creeper passes, all the grass kneels.

27. What goes in the water black and comes out red?

28. Iron roofs, glass walls, burns and burns and never falls.

29. You can only have it once you have given it.

30. What can you fold but not crease?

31. I bind it and it walks. I lose it and it stops.

32. I have a tongue but cannot taste. I have a soul but cannot feel. What am I?

33. We are five little objects of an everyday sort; you will find us all in a tennis court.

34. To unravel me, you need a key. No key that was made by locksmith's hand, but a key that only I will understand. What am I?

35. I can always go up, never down, I can always turn left, never right, I am always hot when I'm cold.

36. I don't exist unless you cut me, but if you stab me, I won't bleed. I hate no one yet am abhorred by all. What am I?

37. I do not listen to reason, but I hear every siren's song and will try to steer us towards the rocks if you let me take the wheel. Who am I?

38. I am something all men have but all men deny. Man created me but no man can hold me. What am I?

39. I cannot be other than what I am, Until the

man who made me dies, Power and glory will fall to me finally, only when he last closes his eyes.

40. I saw a man in white, he looked quite a sight. He was not old, but he stood in the cold. And when he felt the sun, he started to run. Who could he be? Please answer me.

41. A hundred brothers lie next to each other; Each white and fine – they've only one spine. I am the tongue that lies between two. Remove me to gathertheirwisdomtoyou.

42. For our ambrosia we were blessed, By Jupiter, with a sting of death. Though our might, to some is jest, we have quelled the dragon's breath. Who arewe?

43. What must be in the oven yet cannot be

baked? Grows in the heat yet shuns the light of day? What sinks in water but rises with air? Looks like skin,butisfineashair?

44. I dig out tiny caves, and store gold and silver in them. I also build bridges of silver and make crowns of gold. They are the smallest you could imagine.Soonerorlater, everybody needs my help, yet many people are afraid to let me help them. Who am I?

45. What is put on a table, cut, but never eaten?

46. Slayer of regrets, old and new, sought by many, found by few.

47. I ate one and threw away two.

48. Kills the bad ones and the sad ones. Tightens to fit, so one size fits.

49. Break it and it is better, immediately set and harder to break again.

50. An open-ended barrel, it is shaped like a hive. It is filled with the flesh, and the flesh is alive!

51. Two legs I have, and this will confound, only at rest do they touch the ground. What am I?

52. A deep well full of knives

53. We hurt without moving. We poison without touching. We bear the truth and the lies. We are not to be judged by our size. What are we?

54. The strangest creature you'll ever find: Two eyes in front and many-many more behind.

55. I cover what is real and hide what is true, but sometimes I bring out the courage in you. What am I?

56. I'm so simple I only point, Yet I guide people all over the world. What am I?

57. Goes over all the hills and hollows, Bites hard, but never swallows.

58. What is that which goes with a carriage, comes with a carriage, is of no use to a carriage, and yet the carriage cannot go without it?

59. Thousand layup gold within this house, but no man made it. Spears past counting

guard this house, but no man wards it.

60. I cut through evil Like a double-edged sword, and chaos flees at my approach. Balance I single-handedly upraise, through battles fought with heart and mind,Instead of with my gaze. What am I?

61. No head has he but he wears a hat. No feet have he but he stands up straight. On him perhaps a fairy sat, weaving a spell one evening late!

62. What has everything inside it? Everything you can imagine even god, wind, world, sky, heaven, earth and everything that comes to your mind?

63. Above the kingdom I reign, Spotted, speckled, with a mane, I travel in packs, and if you're lucky, you'd ride me. What am I?

64. I am made from an animal, although you nickname me after a different one. You can't eat me; you can only hold me, and once a year a festival is erected in my

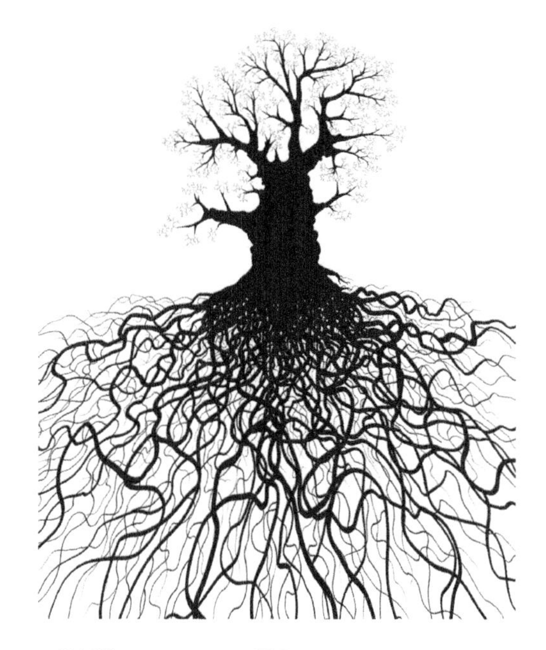

honor. What am I?

65. What grows in winter, dies in summer, and

grows roots upward?

66. Downward grows the root. Outward grows the skin. Upward grows the shoot. What way blows the wind?

67. Shorter than my four siblings, but easily the strongest, Sometimes I wear a funny hat.

68. With head without hair. With mouth without tooth.

69. What flies around all day but never goes anywhere?

70. What's as small as a mouse but guards a

house like a lion?

71. **What gets whiter the dirtier that it gets?**

72. **On the wall, in the air, you just want me out of your hair, try to catch me, but you cannot, for my vision is thousand-fold. What am I?**

73. **I am born in fear, raised in truth, And I come to my own in deed. When comes a time that I'm called forth, I come to serve the cause of need.**

74. **I am slim and tall Many find me desirable and appealing They touch me and I give a false good feeling Once I shine in splendor but only once and then nomore for manyI am to die for. What am I?**

75. **A little pool with two layers of wall around**

it. One white and soft and the other dark and hard, amidst a light brown grassy lawn with an outline ofa greengrass.What am I?

76. Looks like water, but it's heat. Sits on sand, lays on concrete. People have been known, to follow it everywhere. But it gets them no place, and alltheycan doisstare.

77. You use me for multiple reasons, I am many colored, and many shaped. I may or may not also tell you your sexual preference. What am I?

78. My thunder comes before my lightning. My

lightning comes before my rain. And my rain dries all the ground it touches. What am I?

79. I come when the weather is at its prime, Though, it might be wise to leave nothing on the street. But, in the wintertime My name is obsolete What amI?

80. Useful tools for who in darkness dwell. Within you, corrupting like a deadly spell.

81. A leathery snake, with a stinging bite, I'll stay coiled up, Unless I must fight.

82. I'm a bearer of darkness. I'm feared and often hated. I'm a symbol of the unwanted, an omen that leaves you jaded. Some people can predict my coming, butthen you'llforever see Things lurking around corners... Are you sure that it was me?

83. Black we are and much admired, Men seek us if they are tired, we tire the horse, comfort man, Guess this riddle if you can.

84. My step is slow, the snow's my breath I give the ground, a grinding death My marching makes an end of me Slain by sun or drowned in sea.

85. If your life is cut short, I am not the one to blame. You signed up, and your death was not my aim. Enter our doors; there is so much to see, we just happentohold the key, to adventure abound and fun to be found Step in our door and see what is in store. What am I?

86. What has roots that nobody sees, is taller than trees, Up, up it goes, yet it never grows?

87. A natural state, I'm sought by all. Go with me and you shall fall. You do me when you spend, and you use me when you eat to no end. What am I?

88. At the sound of me, men may dream or stamp their feet at the sound of me, women may laugh or sometimes weep.

89. When set loose, I fly away, never so cursed, as when I go astray

90. Early ages the iron boot tread, With Europe at her command. Through time power slipped and fled, 'til the creation of new holy land. Who am I?

91. Armless, legless, I crawl around when I'm young. Then the time of changing sleep will come. I will awake like a newborn, flying beast, 'till then ontheremainsofthe dead I feast.

92. With my pair I should be, But I am usually alone you see, for a monster always eats me. Do you know what I must be?

93. Shifting, Shifting, Drifting deep. Below me great and mighty cities sleep. Swirling, Sculling, All around. I'm only where no water will be found.

94. We are emeralds and diamonds, lost by the moon; Found by the sun, and picked up soon.

95. What is red and nailed to a wall?

96. What has 3 feet but cannot walk?

97. What can an elephant and a shrimp both be?

98. What is given but kept by the giver?

99. The stack just might be sent all over. Full of what's new, yet it's nearly obsolete.

100. I'm tall when I'm young and I'm short when I'm old. What am I?

101. I'm light as a feather, yet the strongest man can't hold me for more than 5 minutes. What am I?

102. I come in many colors, some are blue and white. While some people annoy me, I am not much for the fight. I live where people rarely tread, but you will find me close to

bed. What am I?

103. Sometimes I am light, sometimes I am dark. What am I?

104. I have a hundred legs but cannot stand, a long neck but no head; I eat the maid's life. What am I?

105. I can sizzle like bacon, I am made with an egg, I have plenty of backbone, but lack a good leg. I peel layers like onions, but still remain whole. I can be long like a flagpole, yet fit in a hole. What am I?

106. I build up castles. I tear down mountains. I make some men blind; I help others to see. What am I?

107. I have a tongue, but cannot speak. I have a bed but cannot sleep. I have four legs but

cannot walk. Yet I move as you do. What am I?

108. A hill full, a hole full; yet you cannot catch a bowl full. What is it?

109. Big as a biscuit, deep as a cup, but even a river can't fill it up. What is it?

110. What is it something that you always have but you always leave behind?

111. What is it that makes tears without sorrow and takes its journey to heaven?

112. Round like a dishpan and smaller than a bathtub. But the ocean can't fill it. What is it?

113. A mile from end to end, yet as close to as a friend. A precious commodity, freely given. Seen on the dead and on the living. Found on the rich, poor, short and tall, but shared among children most of all. What is it?

114. Born at the same time as the world, destined to live as long as the world, and yet never five weeks old. What is it?

115. What has wings, but cannot fly. Is enclosed, but can outside also lie. Can open itself up, Or close itself away. Is the place of kings and queens, And doggerel of every means? What is it upon which I stand? Which can lead us to different lands.

116. A mother had five boys Marco, Tucker, Webster and Thomas. Was the fifth boys name Frank, Evan or Alex?

117. A pet shop owner had a parrot with a sign on its cage that said "Parrot repeats everything it hears." A young man bought the parrot and for two weeks he spoke to it and it didn't say a word. He returned the parrot but the shopkeeper said he never lied about the parrot. How can this be?

118. In the land of the green glass door there are riddles but no answers, sheets but no blankets, and books but no words. Name something found in the land of the green glass door.

119. There is a clothing store in Bartlesville. The owner has devised his own method of pricing items. A vest costs $20, socks cost $25, a tie costs $15 and a blouse costs $30.

Using the method, how much would a pair of underwear cost?

120. If you're 8 feet away from a door and with each move you advance half the distance to the door. How many moves will it take to reach the door?

121. I never was, am always to be, No one ever saw me, nor ever will, and yet I am the confidence of all, to live and breathe on this terrestrial ball. Who am I?

122. It's been around for millions of years, but is never more than a month old. What is it?

123. It's been around for millions of years, but is never more than a month old. What is it?

124. There was a little heart inside a little white house, which was inside a little yellow

house, which was inside a little brown house, which was inside a little green house.

125. I cannot be bought, cannot be sold, even if I'm sometimes made of gold. What am I?

126. Although glory but not at my best. Power will fall to me finally, when the man made me is dead. What am I?

127. I am an English word with 3 consecutive double letters. What am I?

128. It stands on one leg with its heart in its head. What is it?

129. As your ideas grow, I shrink. What am I?

130. What's higher than the king?

131. To unravel me you need a simple key, no key that was made by locksmith's hand. But a key that only I will understand.

132. Toss me out of the window. You'll find a grieving wife. Pull me back but through the door, and watch someone give life.

133. My back and belly are wood, and my ribs is lined with leather. I've a hole in my nose and one in my breast, And I'm mostly used in cold weather.

134. I can honk without using a horn. What am I?

135. I have two hands but cannot clap

136. A precious fluid, thicker than water.

137. I am a mother from a family of eight. Spins

around all day despite my weight. Had a ninth sibling before finding out its fake. What am I?

138. Where do sailors take their baths?

139. What is made of wood but can't be sawed?

140. A young lady walked through the meadow and scattered her glass pearls. The Moon saw this, yet didn't tell her. The Sun woke up and gathered the pearls.

141. Gets rid of bad ones, short and tall. Tightens when used, one size fits all.

142. Inside a great blue castle lives a shy young maid. She blushes in the morning and

comes not out at night.

143. I stand up tall and made of steel, with baguettes and garlic at my heel. I love the colors red, white and blue, but obviously not as much as you. I am a marvel for all to see, though to some I am a monstrosity! What am I?

144. Where do cows go to dance?

145. It's a game played by serious people that takes place on a global scale.

146. The more you take of me, the more you leave behind. What am I?

147. A dagger thrust at my own heart; dictates the way I'm swayed. Left I stand, and right I yield, to the twisting of the blade.

148. **Bury deep, Pile on stones, my mind will always Dig up them bones**

149. **It hisses but it's not a snake. It holds water but it's not a lake. When it's done you hear it scream. Pour from it and add some cream.**

150. **This small creature kills even the largest one.**

151. **Never resting, never still. Moving silently from hill to hill. It does not walk, run or trot. All is cool where it is not.**

152. **Its tail is round and hollow, seems to get chewed a bit, but you'll rarely see this thing Unless the other end is lit.**

153. **Whoever makes it, tells it not. Whoever takes it, knows it not. Whoever knows it,**

wants it not. What am I?

154. I am weightless, but you can see me. Put me in a bucket, and I'll make it lighter. What am I?

155. I'm the start of eternity and the end of space. There are two of me in heaven and one in hell.

156. What liquid can contain the soul?

157. What liquid can contain the soul?

158. It speaks without a tongue, and listens without ears.

159. You need a key to receive an answer from me. The answer you'll find is straight from your mind. What is it?

160. I am everywhere but cannot be seen, captured or held, only heard. What am I?

161. What gets beaten, and whipped, but never cries?

162. Sitting down you have it, standing up you don't.

163. I hold two people together but touch only one. What am I?

164. I am a window, I am a lamp, I am clouded, I am shining, I am colored and set in white, I fill with water and overflow. I say much, but I have no words.

165. This is your stomach's way of letting you know you've neglected it.

166. This is your stomach's way of letting you know you've neglected it.

167. I tremble at each breath of air, and yet can heaviest burdens bear.

168. What covers its face with its hands, speaks no language, yet most known what it's saying?

169. I give life for my own, have a beginning, but my end is unknown. What am I?

170. I make you weak at the worst of all times. I keep you safe, I keep you fine. I make your hands sweat. And your heart grows cold. I visit the weak, but seldom the bold.

171. Soldiers line up spaced with pride. Two long rows lined side by side. One sole unit can decide, if the rows will unite or divide.

172. **Has no feet, but travels far. Is literate, but not a scholar. Has no mouth, yet clearly**

speaks.

173. **Comes in bits and pieces, put together forms a whole. It's athletics for the mind, the more you think the more you find. Sometimes it can be a grind, but then, that is the goal.**

174. **I am the ultimate killing machine, used not once but TWICE, I can be made by humans. What am I?**

175. A muttered rumble was heard from the pen, and I, in my walking stopped to look in. What was this I saw? A massive beast, hoofed, and jawed. With spikes upon its mighty brow, I watched as he struck the turf and prowled. And yet for all of his magnificence, he couldn't get out of that wooden fence.

176. Men seize it from its home, tear apart its flesh, drink the sweet blood, then cast its skin aside.

177. One of the few times it's encouraged to lock lips with a stranger.

178. Though it is not an ox, it has horns; Though it is not a donkey, it has packed-saddle; And wherever it goes it leaves silver behind.

179. What animal has feet on the head?

180. A house full, a yard full, a chimney full, no one can get a spoonful.

181. What is between heaven and earth?

182. A thousand colored folds stretch toward the sky. Atop a tender strand, rising from the land, until killed by maiden's hand. Perhaps a token of love, perhaps to say goodbye.

183. To give me to someone I don't belong to is cowardly, but to take me is noble. I can be a game, but there are no winners. What am I?

184. What has two spines and a lot of ribs, and carries much but never moves?

185. When I get closer my tail grows longer, but when I go away my tail leads the way.

186. **Fighting technique taken from rams.**

187. **Stealthy as a shadow in the dead of night, cunning but affectionate if given a bite. Never owned but often loved. At my sport considered cruel, but that's because you never know me at all.**

188. **Crooked as a rainbow, and slick as a plate,**

ten thousand horses can't pull it straight.

189. **Currency that flirted with a British spy.**

190. Has feathers but can't fly. Rests on legs but can't walk.

191. What is deep within you, never dies or gets worn out, and only needs some fire from time to time?

192. Locked up inside you and yet they can steal it from you.

193. This is the tallest peak in the happiest place on earth.

194. My parents are singers, and while my father has red hair, I am pale and completely bald.

195. I may be made of metal, bone, or wood and have many teeth. My bite hurts no one and the ladies love me. What am I?

196. **Green arrows grow out of my sides. I go from yellow to white. My babies fly in the wind. What am I?**

197. **I have no voice but I can teach you all there is to know. I have spines and hinges but I am not a door. Once I've told you all, I cannot tell you more. What am I?**

198. **Sharp and long, flag of the world. What is it?**

199. I cannot be felt or moved, but as you come closer, I get more distant. What am I?

200. With no hammer or any kind of tool I build my house so quickly. What am I?

201. Some live in me, some live on. And some shave me to stride upon. I rarely leave my native land. Until my death I always stand. High and low I may be found. Both above and below ground.

202. It is greater than God and more evil than the devil. The poor have it, the rich need it, and if you eat it, you'll die.

203. Ripped from my mother's womb. Beaten and burned, I become a bloodthirsty killer. What am I?

204. Face with a tree, skin like the sea. A great beast I am. Yet vermin frighten me.

205. What is round on both ends and hi in the middle?

206. Everybody has some. You can lose some, you can gain some. But you cannot live without it. What am I?

207. In Paris but not in France, the thinnest of its siblings.

208. I don't think or eat or slumber. Or move around or fear thunder. Just like you I look the same but I can't harm you or be your bane.

209. If you agree give me one of these.

210. The more you look at it, the less you see.

211. What fruit is of great use in history?

212. All about the house, with his lady he dances, yet he always works, and never romances.

213. I may seem real but it always turns out. I was never there in the first place... You only see me during a certain resting stage. What am I?

214. He died for people's entertainment.

215. Covered in stone and sun. It's home to many but also none. What is it?

216. **I encourage people to run home and steal. What am I?**

217. **What is that which, though black itself, enlightens the world without burning?**

218. **It is a part of us, and then replaced. It escapes our bodies, to a better place. The world becomes its sizeable home. Its passions unrestrained, the planet it roams.**

219. **You may have to assure your date's dad that**

you have these kinds of intentions.

220. Has its teeth on your head but doesn't bite.

221. What two things can you never have for breakfast?

222. What is so fragile that saying its name breaks it?

223. What can run but never walks, has a mouth but never talks, has a head but never weeps, has a bed but never sleeps?

224. What can fill a room but takes up no space?

225. If you drop me I'm sure to crack, but give me a smile and I'll always smile back. What am I?

226. What is the capital in France?

227. The more you take, the more you leave behind. What are they?

228. I turn once, what is out will not get in.
I turn again, what is in will not get out.
What am I?

229. A man calls his dog from the opposite side of the river. The dog crosses the river without getting wet, and without using a bridge or boat. How?

230. What breaks yet never falls, and what falls yet never breaks?

231. What goes through cities and fields, but never moves?

232. I am always hungry and will die if not fed, but whatever I touch will soon turn red. What am I?

233. The person who makes it has no need of it; the person who buys it has no use for it. The person who uses it can neither see nor feel it. What is it?

234. A man looks at a painting in a museum and says, "Brothers and sisters I have none, but that man's father is my father's son." Who is in the painting?

235. With pointed fangs I sit and wait; with piercing force I crunch out fate; grabbing victims, proclaiming might; physically joining with a single bite. What am I?

236. I have lakes with no water, mountains with no stone and cities with no buildings. What am I?

237. What does man love more than life, hate more than death or mortal strife; that which contented men desire; the poor have, the rich require; the miser spends, the spendthrift saves, and all men carry to their graves?

238. Mr. and Ms. Mustard have six daughters and each daughter has one brother. How many people are in the Mustard family?

239. I am something people love or hate. I change people's appearances and thoughts. If a person takes care of themself, I will go up even higher. Some people might want to try and hide me but I will show. No matter how hard people try I will never go down. What am I?

240. Only one color, but not one size,Stuck at the bottom, yet easily flies. Present in sun, but not in rain,doing no harm, and feeling no pain. What is it?

241. Who is that with a neck and no head, two arms and no hands?

242. If eleven plus two equals one, what does nine plus five equal?

243. Can you write down eight eights so that they add up to one thousand?

244. It can't be seen, can't be felt, can't be heard, and can't be smelt. It lies behind stars and under hills, And empty holes it fills. It comes first and follows after, Ends life, and kills laughter. What is it?

245. What English word retains the same

pronunciation, even after you take away four of its five letters?

246. Three playing cards in a row. Can you name them with these clues? There is a two to the right of a king. A diamond will be found to the left of a spade. An ace is to the left of a heart. A heart is to the left of a spade. Now, identify all three cards

247. What is it that given one, you'll have either two or none?

248. George, Helen, and Steve are drinking coffee. Bert, Karen, and Dave are drinking soda. Using logic, is Elizabeth drinking coffee or soda?

249. I have branches, yet I have no leaves, no trunk, and no fruit. What am I?

250. What has a head, a tail, is brown, and has no legs?

251. When I'm used, I'm useless. Once offered, soon rejected. In desperation, I'm oft expressed. What am I?

252. I have four legs, but no hair. People ride me for hours, but don't go anywhere. Without needing to be tugged or turned on, I always manage to be ready for work. What am I?

253. Which of the following words don't belong in the group and why? CORSET, COSTER, SECTOR, ESCORT, COURTS

254. When John was six years old he hammered a nail into his favorite tree to mark his height. Ten years later at age sixteen, John returned to see how much higher the nail was. If the tree grew by five centimeters

each year, how much higher would the nail be?

255. **I am four times as old as my daughter. In 20 years time I shall be twice as old as her. How old are we now?**

256. **There was a man who was born before his father, killed his mother, and married his sister. Yet, there was nothing wrong with what he had done. Why?**

257. **Lily is a lilypad in a small pond. Lily doubles her size each day, On the 20th day she covers the whole pond. On what day was Lily half the size of the pond?**

258. **What common English verb becomes its own past tense by rearranging its letters?**

259. **When asked how old she was, Suzie replied, "In two years I will be twice as old as I was five years ago." How old is she?**

260. **Lighter than what I am made of, More of me is hidden Than is seen. What am I?**

261. **It's shorter than the rest but when you're happy you raise it up like it's the best. What is it?**

262. **The man who bought it doesn't want it for himself. The man who buys it doesn't buy it for himself. And the man who needs it doesn't know he needs it. What is it?**

263. **I have cities, but no houses. I have mountains, but no trees. I have water, but**

no fish. What am I?

264. A girl has as many brothers as sisters, but each brother has only half as many brothers as sisters. How many brothers and sisters are there in the family?

265. A girl has as many brothers as sisters, but each brother has only half as many brothers as sisters. How many brothers and sisters are there in the family?

266. Different lights do make me strange, thus into different sizes I will change. What am I

267. What has a tail and a head but no body?

268. I am an odd number. Take away a letter and I become even. What number am I?

269. If a red house is made of red bricks, and a yellow house is made of yellow bricks, what is a greenhouse made of?

270. What can never be put in a saucepan?

271. What can run but never walks, has a mouth but never talks, has a head but never weeps, has a bed but never sleeps?

272. Two fathers and two sons went on a fishing trip. Each of them caught a fish. There were three fish caught in total. How is this possible?

273. You can find me in Earth, Mars, Mercury, and Jupiter - but not Venus, Pluto, or Neptune. What am I?

274. They get me from a mine and shut me inside a wooden case. I am never released, and almost everybody uses me. What am I?

275. If 11 + 2 = 1, then what does 9 + 5 =?

276. What is really easy to get into, but very difficult to get out of?

277. There is an English word that is pronounced the same even when you remove away four of the five letters. What is it?

278. I am not alive, but I can grow. I don't have any lungs, but I need air to survive. I don't have a mouth, but water kills me. What am I?

279. Forward I'm heavy, backward I'm not. What am ?

280. **A man has a bee in his hand. What's in his eye?**

281. **A man wants to enter an exclusive club, but he doesn't know the password, so he watches the bouncer to figure it out. A woman comes up and the bouncer says, "12." The woman replies, "6." The bouncer lets her in. Another woman comes up and the bouncer says, "6." The woman says "3" and the bouncer lets her in. The man feels he's heard enough and goes up to the door. The bouncer says "10," and the man replies, "5." The bouncer tells him to get lost. What should the man have said instead?**

282. **Tear one off and scratch my head. What once was red is black instead. What am I?**

283. **What tastes better than it smells?**

284. **When you need me you throw me away. When you don't need me you bring me back. What am I?**

285. **If you throw me out a window, you'll leave a grieving wife. Bring me back, but through the door, and give someone a new life. What am I?**

286. **Five hundred begins it, five hundred ends it, five in the middle is seen. The first of all leters and the first of all numbers take the spaces between. Now put it together and you will discover the name of a once-famous king. Who is it?**

287. **Imagine you're in a dark room with no windows and a locked door. How do you get out?**

288. **You leave home running. You make a right, then turn left twice. You turn left one more time and see two men in masks. Who are they?**

289. **I'm light as a feather, but the longer you hold me, the harder I am to keep. What am I?**

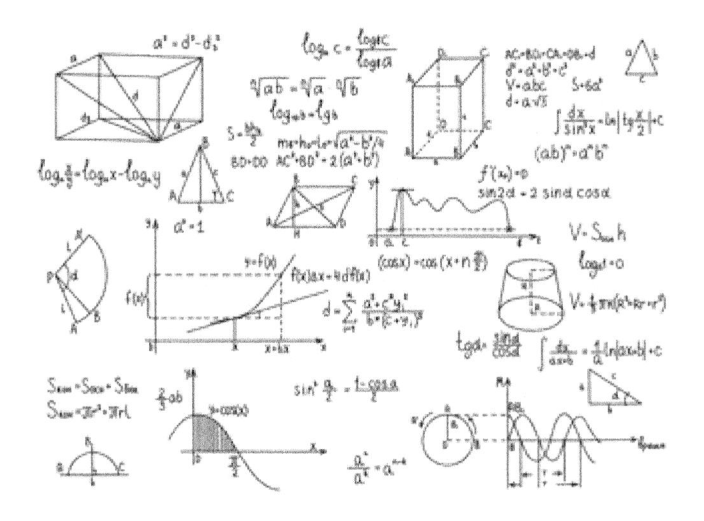

290. **We are all very little creatures; all of us have different features. One of us in glass is set; One of us you'll find in jet. Another you may see in tin, And a fourth is boxed within. If the fifth you should pursue, It can never fly from you. What are we?**

291. 1 is 3. 2 is 3. 3 is 5. What is 4?

292. A murderer is condemned to death. He is given the choice between three rooms. The first room is full of raging fires. The second is full of assassins with loaded guns. The third is full of lions that haven't eaten in 3 years. Which room should he choose?

293. Two fathers and their two sons go hunting in the woods. They each shoot a rabbit and bring it home. They don't lose any rabbits but only have three when they arrive. How is that possible?

294. Whoever makes me tells me not. Whoever takes me, knows me not. Whoever knows me, want me not. What am I?

295. I am something people love or hate. I change people's appearances and

thoughts. If a person takes care of themself, I will go up even higher. To some people, I will fool them. To others, I am a mystery. Some people might want to try and hide me, but I will show. No matter how hard people try, I will never go down. What am I?

296. What can you hold in your right hand but not your left?

297. An old man dies, leaving behind two sons. In his will, he orders his sons to race with their horses, and the one with the slower horse will receive his inheritance. The two sons race, but since they're both holding their horses back, they go to a wise man and ask him what they should do. After that, the brothers race again — this time at full speed. What did the wise man tell them?

298. There are three chests, each of which contains 100 coins. One chest has 100 gold coins, one has 100 silver coins, and the third has an equal split of 50 gold coins and 50 silver coins. Each chest is labelled, but all are mislabeled. You are allowed to pick one coin from just one of the cases, and after this, you must correctly identify each of the three chests. What should you do?

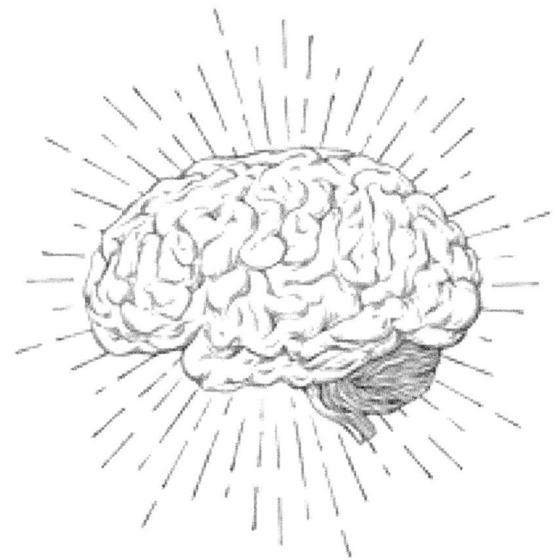

299. You should keep me as straight as can be, yet very few do. Most of the time, I am slightly bent or curved. Your sadness usually causes me to bend further, but don't bend me for too long, or I may never

be able to straighten out again fully. What am I?

300. I move very slowly at an imperceptible rate, although I take my time, I am never late. I accompany life and survive past demise; I am viewed with esteem in many women's eyes. What am I?

DIFFICULT MATH RIDDLES

1. If there are 4 apples and you take away 3, how many do you have?

2. A 300 ft. train is traveling 300 ft. per minute must travel through a 300 ft. long tunnel. How long will it take the train to travel through the tunnel?

3. A cellphone and a phone case cost $110 in total. The cell phone costs $100 more than the phone case. How much was the cellphone?

4. Robert and David played several golf matches against each other in a week. They played for a pizza at each match, but no pizzas were purchased until the end of the week. If at any time Robert and David had the same number of wins, those pizzas were canceled. Robert won four matches (but no pizzas), and David won three pizzas. How many rounds of golf were played?

5. I am a three-digit number. My second digit is 4 times bigger than the third digit. My first digit is 3 less than my second digit. Who am I?

6. I add five to nine, and get two. The answer is

correct, but how?

7.There are 100 pairs of dogs in a zoo; pairs of babies are born for every dog. Unfortunately, 23 of the dogs have not survived. How many dogs would be left in total?

8.A group of students were standing in the blazing sun facing due west on a march past event. The leader shouted at them: Right turn! About turn! Left turn! At the end of these commands, in which direction is the students facing now?

9.A half is a third of it. What is it?

10.At the time of shipping, Tom can place 10 small boxes or 8 large boxes into a carton. A total of 96 boxes were sent in one shipment. The number of small boxes was less than large boxes. What is the total number of cartons he shipped?

11.When Miguel was 6 years old, his little sister, Leila, was half is age. If Miguel is 40 years old today, how old is Leila?

12.You are given 3 positive numbers. You can add these numbers and multiply them together. The result you get will be the

same. Which are the numbers?

13. **If a hen and a half lay an egg and a half in a day and a half, how many eggs will half a dozen hens lay in half a dozen days?**

14. **What can you put between a 7 and an 8 so that the result is greater than a seven, but less than an eight?**

15. **Tom was asked to paint the numbers outside 100 apartments which means he will have to paint numbers 1 through 100. Can you figure out the number of times he will have to paint the number 8?**

16. **What's the maximum number of times you can subtract number 5 from 25?**

17. **Which weighs more 16 ounces of soda or a pound of solid gold?**

18. **Leon works at the aquarium. When he tries to put each turtle in its own tank, he has one turtle too many. But if he puts two turtles per tank, he has on tank too many. How many turtles and how many tanks does Leon have?**

19. **The total cost of a pair of shoes and a hoodie is $150. The hoodie costs $100 more**

than the pair of shoes does. How much does each item cost?

20.You have two U.S coins whose total value is $0.30. One of them is not a nickel. What are the two coins?

21.Eggs are $0.12 a dozen. How many eggs can you get for a dollar?

22.A duck was given $9, a spider was given $36, a bee was given $27. Based on this information, how much money would be given to a cat?

23."How much is this bag of potatoes?" asked the man. "32 pounds divided by half of its own weight," said the grocer. How much did the potatoes weigh?

24.I am a three-digit number. My tens digit is six more than my ones digit. My hundreds digit is eight less than my tens digit. What number am I?

25.A man is twice as old as his little sister. He is also half as old as his dad. Over a period of 50 years, the age of his sister will become half of their dad's age. What is the age of the man now?

26. **How can you add eight 4s together so that the total adds up to 500?**

27. **If seven people meet each other and each shake hands only once with each of the others, how many handshakes will there have been?**

28. **If four men can build four tables in four hours, how many tables can eight men build in eight hours?**

29. **When Lisa was 6 years old, her sister Lucy was half her age. If Lucy is 40 years old today, how old is Lucy?**

30. **If you buy a rooster for the purpose of laying eggs and you expect to get three eggs each day for breakfast, how many eggs will you have after three weeks?**

31. **A farmer has 19 sheep on his land. One day, a big storm hits, and all but seven run away. How many sheep does the farmer have left?**

HARD PUZZLES

1. Two people are playing chess. According to the results of five games, each player scored three wins. How could this happen?

2. Would you guess which letter is missing here?

3.

HOW MANY HOLES DOES THE T-SHIRT HAVE?

IT'S NOT 2.

4. Which patterned block goes in the fourth spot?

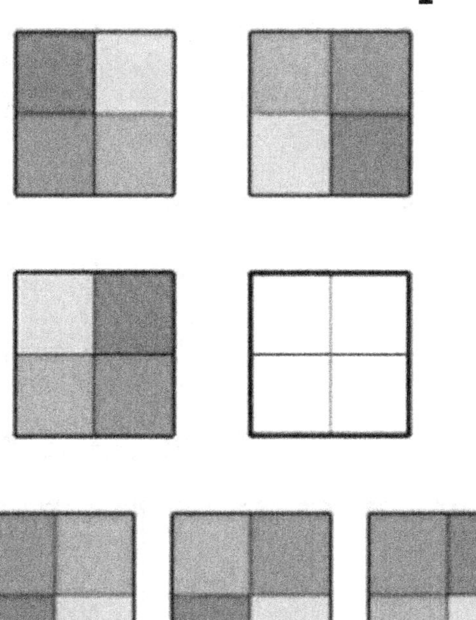

a b c d

5. How many blocks in this tower?

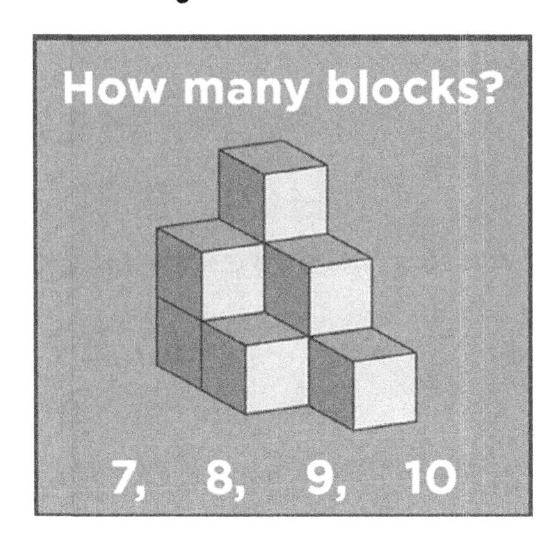

6. How many blocks in this tower?

Which is the correct net to form the given cube ?

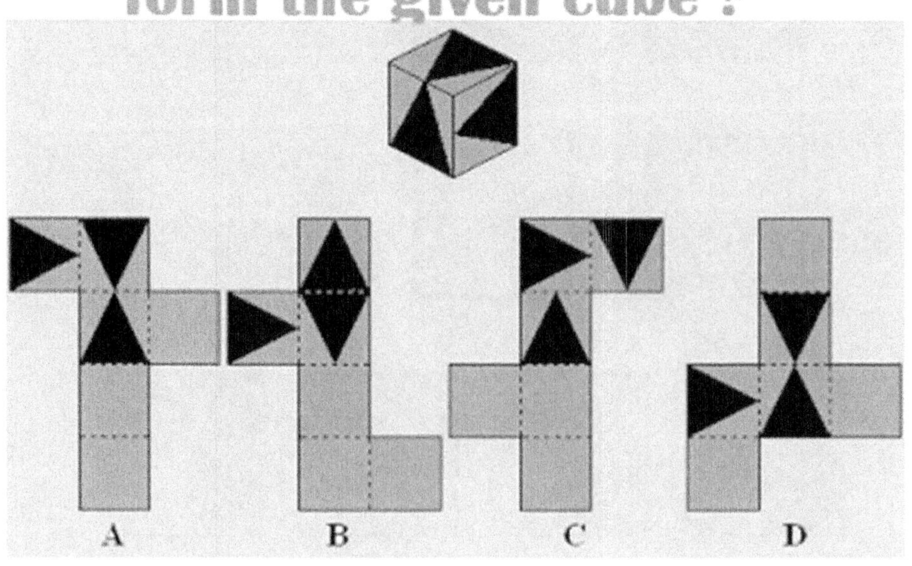

7. How many triangles there are in the image.

8. how many squares they can see.

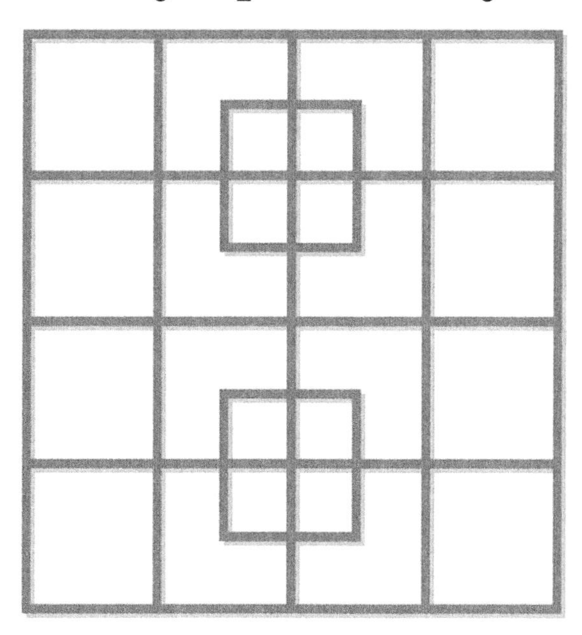

9. You can see three glasses on the left that are full, and three on the right that are empty. You can only move one glass to make a row of alternately full and empty glasses. Which one do you move?

10. need to remove 6 matches to make 10. Which ones do they move?

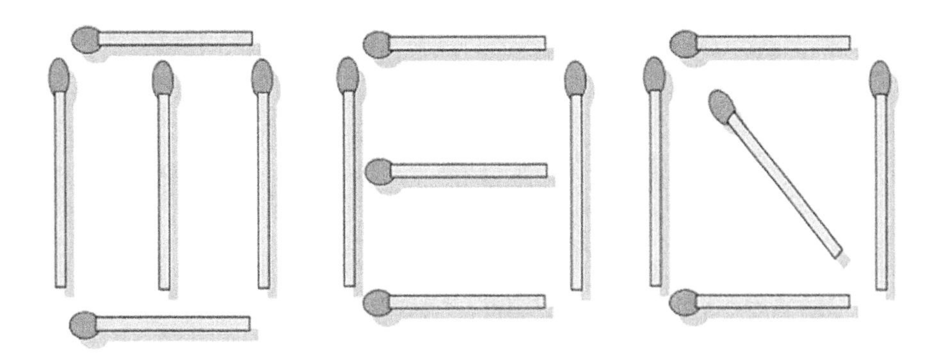

11.

What is the number of the parking space containing the car?

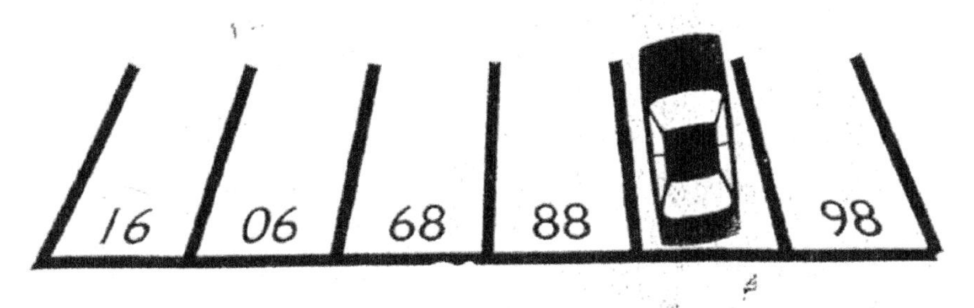

12. What is our weight?

DIFFICULT RIDDLES ANSWERS

1. *TEMPER*
2. *CARPET*
3. *STAPLER*
4. *RULER*
5. *BACON*
6. *HYPNOTISM*
7. *JAR*
8. *STEPS*
9. *BANANA*
10. *CHISEL*
11. *BEADS*

12. *LAP*

13. *DANDELION*

14. *WISDOM*

15. *CABBAGE*

16. *RISK*

17. *TEA BAG*

18. *SACK*

19. *DOCTOR*

20. *CANNON*

21. *GRUDGE*

22. *ZEBRA*

23. *SEESAW*

24. *SPURS*

25. *FOUNTAIN*

26. *PLOW*

27. *LOBSTER*

28. *LANTERN*

29. *RESPECT*

30. *POKER HAND*

31. *SANDAL*

32. *SHOE*

33. *VOWELS*

34. *CIPHER*

35. *SKI LIFT*

36. *FART*

37. *FART*

38. *FEAR*

39. *PRINCE*

40. *SNOWMAN*

41. *BOOKMARK*

42. *BEES*

43. *YEAST*

44. *DENTIST*

45. *CARDS*

46. *REDEMPTION*

47. *OYSTER*

48. *NOOSE*

49. *RECORD*

50. *THIMBLE*

51. *WHEELBARROW*

52. *MOUTH*

53. *WORDS*

54. *PEACOCK*

55. *MAKEUP*

56. *COMPASS*

57. *FROST*

58. *NOISE*

59. *BEEHIVE*

60. *JUSTICE*

61. *TOADSTOOL*

62. *ALPHABET*

63. *GIRAFFE*

64. *FOOTBALL*

65. *ICICLE*

66. *WAYWARD*

67. *THUMB*

68. *BOTTLE*

69. *FLAG*

70. *LOCK*

71. *CHALKBOARD*

72. *FLY*

73. *COURAGE*

74. *CIGARETTE*

75. *COCONUT*

76. *MIRAGE*

77. *SCARF*

78. *VOLCANO*

79. *HAIL*

80. *POISON*

81. *WHIP*

82. *GRIM*

83. *COAL*

84. *GLACIER*

85. *TERROR TOURS*

86. *MOUNTAIN*

87. *BALANCE*

88. *MUSIC*

89. *RAFT*

90. *ROME*

91. *MAGGOT*

92. *SOCKS*

93. *DESERT*

94. *DEW*

95. *HERRING*

96. *YARDSTICK*

97. *JUMBO*

98. *BIRTH*

99. *NEWSPAPERS*

100. *CANDLE*

101. *BREATH*

102. *WHALES*

103. *CHOCOLATE*

104. *BROOM*

105. *SNAKE*

106. *SAND*

107. *WAGON*

108. *MIST*

109. *STRAINER*

110. *FINGERPRINTS*

111. *SMOKE*

112. *SIEVE*

113. *SMILE*

114. *MOON*

115. *STAGE*

116. *THE ANSWER IS FRANK. EACH CHILD'S FIRST NAME BEGINS WITH THE FIRST LETTERS OF THE DAYS OF THE WEEK M, T, W, T, FRANK.*

117. *THE PARROT WAS DEAF!*

118. *ANY WORD WITH TWO LETTERS NEXT TO EACH OTHER. LIKE THE WORD LETTERS.*

119. *$45. THE PRICING METHOD CONSISTS OF CHARGING $5 FOR EACH LETTER REQUIRED TO SPELL THE ITEM.*

120. *YOU WILL NEVER REACH THE DOOR, IT WILL ALWAYS BE HALF THE DISTANCE, NO MATTER HOW SMALL!*

121. *TOMORROW*

122. *THE MOON.*

123. *YOUR WORD.*

124. *WALNUT*

125. *HEART*

126. *PRINCE*

127. *BOOKKEEPER*

128. *CABBAGE*

129. *PENCIL*

130. *CROWN*

131. *RIDDLE*

132. *N*

133. *BELLOWS*

134. *GOOSE*

135. *CLOCK*

136. *BLOOD*

137. *EARTH*

138. *TUB MARINE*

139. *SAWDUST*

140. *DEW*

141. *NOOSE*

142. *SUN*

143. *EIFFEL TOWER*

144. *MEATBALL*

145. *POLITICS*

146. *FOOTSTEP*

147. *LOCK*

148. *MEMORIES*

149. *TEAPOT*

150. *BACTERIA*

151. *SUNSHINE*

152. *PIPE*

153. *POISON*

154. *HOLE*

155. *E*

156. *INK*

157. *GRANDFATHER CLOCK*

158. *PHONE*

159. *CODE*

160. *VOICE*

161. *EGG*

162. *LAP*

163. *WEDDING RING*

164. *EYE*

165. *GRUMBLE*

166. *FISH*

167. *WATER*

168. *CLOCK*

169. *SUN*

170. *FEAR*

171. *ZIPPER*

172. *LETTER*

173. *PUZZLE*

174. *WAR*

175. *BULL*

176. *ORANGE*

177. *CPR*

178. *SNAIL*

179. *LICE*

180. *SMOKE*

181. *AND*

182. *FLOWER*

183. *BLAME*

184. *TRAIN TRACKS*

185. *COMET*

186. *HEAD-BUTT*

187. *CAT*

188. *RIVER*

189. *MISS MONEY PENNY*

190. *MATTRESS*

191. *SOUL*

192. *HEART*

193. *MATTERHORN*

194. *EGG*

195. *COMB*

196. *DANDELION*

197. *BOOK*

198. *TOWER*

199. *HORIZON*

200. *SPIDER*

201. *TREE*

202. *NOTHING*

203. *IRON ORE*

204. *ELEPHANT*

205. *OHIO*

206. *BLOOD*

207. *I*

208. *DOLL*

209. *AMEN*

210. *SUN*

211. *DATE*

212. *BROOM*

213. *DREAM*

214. *GLADIATOR*

215. *CEMETERY*

216. *BASEBALL*

217. *INK*

218. *WATER*

219. *HONORABLE*

220. *COMB*

221. *LUNCH AND DINNER*

222. *SILENCE*

223. *A RIVER*

224. *LIGHT*

225. *A MIRROR*

226. *THE LETTER F IS THE ONLY CAPITAL*

LETTER IN FRANCE.

227. *FOOTSTEPS*

228. *A KEY*

229. *THE RIVER WAS FROZEN.*

230. *DAY AND NIGHT*

231. *A ROAD*

232. *FIRE*

233. *A COFFIN*

234. *THE MAN'S SON*

235. *A STAPLER*

236. *A MAP*

237. *NOTHING*

238. *THERE ARE NINE MUSTARDS IN THE*

FAMILY. SINCE EACH DAUGHTER SHARES THE SAME BROTHER, THERE ARE SIX GIRLS, ONE BOY AND MR. AND MS. MUSTARD.

239. *AGE*

240. *A SHADOW*

241. *A SHIRT*

242. *11 O'CLOCK PLUS 2 HOURS = 1 O'CLOCK*
9 O'CLOCK PLUS 5 HOURS = 2 O'CLOCK

243. *888 + 88 + 8 + 8 + 8 = 1000*

244. *THE DARK*

245. *QUEUE*

246. *THREE PLAYING CARDS IN A ROW. CAN YOU NAME THEM WITH THESE CLUES? THERE IS A TWO TO THE RIGHT OF A KING. A DIAMOND WILL BE FOUND TO THE LEFT OF A SPADE. AN ACE IS TO THE LEFT OF A HEART. A HEART IS TO THE*

LEFT OF A SPADE. NOW, IDENTIFY ALL THREE CARDS.

247. *A CHOICE*

248. *ELIZABETH IS DRINKING COFFEE. THE LETTER E APPEARS TWICE IN HER NAME, AS IT DOES IN THE NAMES OF THE OTHERS THAT ARE DRINKING COFFEE.*

249. *A BANK*

250. *A PENNY*

251. *AN EXCUSE*

252. *A DESK*

253. *COURTS. ALL OF THE OTHERS ARE ANAGRAMS OF EACH OTHER.*

254. *THE NAIL WOULD BE AT THE SAME HEIGHT SINCE TREES GROW AT THEIR TOPS*

255. *I AM 40 AND MY DAUGHTER IS 10.*

256. *HIS FATHER WAS IN FRONT OF HIM WHEN HE WAS BORN, THEREFORE HE WAS BORN BEFORE HIM. HIS MOTHER DIED WHILE GIVING BIRTH TO HIM. FINALLY, HE GREW UP TO BE A MINISTER AND MARRIED HIS SISTER AT HER CEREMONY.*

257. *DAY 19, IT'S NOT 10 BECAUSE ON DAY 20 SHE DOUBLED FROM DAY 19, SO 19 MUST BE HALF THE SIZE OF THE POND.*

258. *EAT AND ATE.*

259. *SHE'S 12*

260. *AN ICEBERG.*

261. *A THUMB.*

262. *A COFFIN*

263. *A MAP.*

264. *FOUR SISTERS AND THREE BROTHERS*

265. *WATER*

266. *I AM THE PUPIL OF AN EYE.*

267. *A COIN*

268. *SEVEN*

269. *ALL GREENHOUSES ARE MADE OF GLASS.*

270. *ITS LID*

271. *A RIVER*

272. *THERE WERE ONLY THREE PEOPLE. A GRANDFATHER, A FATHER, AND A SON. THIS EQUALS TWO FATHERS AND TWO SONS.*

273. *THE LETTER R*

274. *PENCIL LEAD*

275. *THIS RIDDLE IS REFERRING TO TIME. 11*

AM + 2 HOURS = 1 PM. 9 PM + 5 HOURS = 2AM

276. *TROUBLE*

277. *QUEUE*

278. *FIRE!*

279. *TON (BECAUSE "NOT" SPELLED BACKWARD IS "TON.")*

280. *BEAUTY (BECAUSE "BEAUTY IS IN THE EYE OF THE BEE-HOLDER.")*

281. *3 — THE NUMBER OF LETTERS IN THE WORD "TEN."*

282. *A MATCH!*

283. *A TONGUE!*

284. *AN ANCHOR*

285. *THE LETTER N. (REMOVE THE LETTER*

"N" FROM "WINDOW" AND YOU GET "WIDOW." PUT THE "N" IN THE WORD "DOOR" AND YOU GET "DONOR.")

286. *DAVID (D IS THE ROMAN NUMERAL FOR 500. V IS THE ROMAN NUMERAL FOR 5. A IS THE FIRST LETTER. I IS THE ROMAN NUMERAL FOR 1 — THE FIRST NUMBER.)*

287. *IMAGINE YOU HAVE THE KEY. (OR STOP IMAGINING THE ROOM!)*

288. *THE CATCHER AND THE UMPIRE. (THEY'RE AT HOME PLATE.)*

289. *YOUR BREATH.*

290. *VOWELS. (HINT: GLASS, JET, TIN, BOXED, YOU.)*

291. *4 IS 4. (ONCE AGAIN, IT'S THE NUMBER OF LETTERS IN THE WORD — 3 IN "ONE," 3 IN "TWO," 5 IN "THREE" AND 4 IN "FOUR.")*

292. *THE ROOM WITH THE LIONS. THEY'RE*

SUPER DEAD.

293. *THERE ARE ONLY THREE MEN — FROM THREE GENERATIONS. A GRANDFATHER, HIS SON, AND HIS GRANDSON.*

294. *COUNTERFEIT MONEY*

295. *AGE*

296. *ELBOW*

297. *ONCE THEY SWITCH HORSES, ANYONE THAT WINS THE RACE WILL RECEIVE THE INHERITANCE AS THEY ARE STILL TECHNICALLY OWN THE LOSING HORSE.*

298. *TAKE A COIN FROM THE CHEST LABELLED 50/50. IF YOU GET A GOLD COIN, YOU ARE GOING TO LEARN THAT THE CHEST POSSESSES GOLD COINS ALONE. THEREFORE, THE ONE MARKED SILVER OUGHT TO BE THE 50/50 CHEST, AND THE ONE LABELLED GOLD IS THE SILVER CHEST.*

299. *YOUR POSTURE.*

300. *I AM YOUR HAIR.*

DIFFICULT MATH RIDDLES ANSWERS

1. *YOU TOOK 3 APPLES, SO YOU HAVE 3!*

2. *TWO MINUTES. IT TAKES THE FRONT OF THE TRAIN ONE MINUTE AND THE REST OF THE TRAIN WILL TAKE TWO MINUTES TO CLEAR THE TUNNEL.*

3. *$105 (NOT $110)*

4. *ELEVEN - Explanation: DAVID WON 7 MATCHES, 4 TO CANCEL OUT ROBERT'S 4 WINS, AND 3 MORE TO WIN THE PIZZAS.*

5. *141*

6. *WHEN IT IS 9AM, ADD 5 HOURS TO IT AND YOU WILL GET TO 2 PM.*

7. *977 DOGS Explanation: 100 X 2 = 200; 200*

+800 = 1000; 1000-23 = 977

8. *EAST. (EXPLANATION: THEY WILL TURN 90 DEGREES IN A RIGHT TURN AND THEY TURN 180 DEGREES IN AN ABOUT-TURN, AND FINALLY THEY TURN 90 DEGREES IN A LEFT-TURN. THEREFORE, THE STUDENTS ARE NOW FACING EAST.)*

9. *1 1/2.*

10. *11 CARTONS (EXPLANATION: 4 SMALL BOXES (410 = 40 BOXES) + 7 LARGE BOXES (78 = 56 BOXES). SO, 96 BOXES AND 11 TOTAL CARTONS.)*

11. *SHE IS 37 YEARS OLD.*

12. *1, 2, AND 3*

13. *2 DOZEN*

14. *A DECIMAL. 7.8 IS GREATER THAN 7, BUT*

LESS THAN 8

15. *20 TIMES (8, 18, 28, 38, 48, 58, 68, 78, 80, 81, 82, 83, 84, 85, 86, 87, 88, 89, 98)*

16. *ONLY ONCE. THIS IS BECAUSE WHEN YOU SUBTRACT 5 FOR THE FIRST TIME, IT BECOMES NUMBER 20, AND THEN 15, AND SO ON.*

17. *NEITHER. THEY BOTH WEIGH THE SAME!*

18. *HE HAS 3 TANKS AND 4 TURTLES.*

19. *THE HOODIE COSTS $125, THE SHOES COSTS $25*

20. *ONE IS A QUARTER AND ONE IS A NICKEL*

21. *100 EGGS, AT A PENNY EACH.*

22. *$18 ($4.50 PER LEG)*

23. *8 LBS.*

24. *193*

25. *50 YEARS OLD.*

26. *444 + 44 + 4 + 4 + 4= 500*

27. *21*

28. *16 TABLES*

29. *37 (EXPLANATION: LUCY IS 3 YEARS YOUNGER THAN LISA.)*

30. *NONE. ROOSTERS DON'T LAY EGGS.*

31. *SEVEN. ALL BUT SEVEN RAN AWAY.*

DIFFICULT PUZZLES ANSWERS

1. *THIS COULD HAPPEN ONLY UNDER ONE CONDITION: IF THEY DID NOT PLAY AGAINST EACH OTHER.*

2. *THIS IS A ROW OF LETTERS THAT LISTS THE FIRST LETTERS OF THE DAYS OF THE WEEK FROM MONDAY TO SUNDAY. SO THE MISSING LETTER IS T.*

3. *THERE ARE 4 HOLES IN THE T-SHIRT, BECAUSE THROUGH THEM WE SEE THE BACKGROUND, MEANING THEY'RE MADE ON BOTH SIDES.*

4. *OPPOSITE SQUARES ARE EXCHANGED IN THIS PROBLEM, SO THE ANSWER IS A.*

5. *THERE ARE 9 BLOCK.*

6. *B AND C CAN BE IMMEDIATELY REJECTED VISUALLY. D WILL CREATE THE MIRROR IMAGE OF THE GIVEN CUBE. SO THE CORRECT ANSWER IS A.*

7. *THERE ARE 44 TRIANGLES.*

8. *THERE ARE 40 SQUARES.*

9. *POUR THE SECOND GLASS FROM THE LEFT INTO THE EMPTY CLASS SECOND FROM THE RIGHT*

10. *YOU CAN MAKE THE WORD 'TEN' BY REMOVING THE BOTTOM MATCHSTICK AND TWO SIDE MATCHSTICKS FROM THE FIRST LETTER. THE FAR RIGHT MATCHSTICK ON THE SECOND LETTER AND THE TOP AND BOTTOM MATCHSTICK ON THE THIRD LETTER.*

11. *TURN THE PICTURE UPSIDE DOWN. YOU WILL THEN SEE THE FOLLOWING NUMBER SEQUENCE: 86 ? 88, 89, 90, 91. SO THE ANSWER IS 87.*

12. *MATHS CALCULATIONS WILL GIVE THE WEIGHT OF THE DOG AS 17 KG. THEREFORE THE WEIGHT OF THE CAT AND RABBIT ARE 10 KG, SO THE ANSWER IS 27 KG.*

THANK YOU FOR PURCHASING THIS BOOK

IF YOU ENJOYED THIS BOOK PLEASE CONSIDER LEAVING AN HONEST REVIEW!!

We will highly appreciate it if you share your thoughts on Amazon about our work.

This motivates us to continue producing quality content and doing everything in our power to help other people and make them happy.

Printed in Great Britain
by Amazon

14005346R00068